50 Crumble Recipes

(50 Crumble Recipes - Volume 1)

Brandy Farr

Content

50 AWESOME CRUMBLE RECIPES 4

1.   4 3 2 1 Crumble Topping.............................4
2.   Ange's Easy Tropical Pineapple Crumble Recipe 4
3.   Apple Crumble 5
4.   Apple Crumble Cake 5
5.   Apple Crumble Custard Hearts Recipe 5
6.   Apple Crumble For Two 6
7.   Apple Crumble Recipe 6
8.   Apple Crumble With Maple Syrup, Walnuts And Oats..7
9.   Apple Crumble With White Choc Bits........7
10.   Apple And Custard ANZAC Bickie Crumble Recipe 7
11.   Appleberry Crumble 8
12.   Banana Cake With Crumble Topping 8
13.   Banana Crumble 9
14.   Banana And Pear Crumble 9
15.   Berry Crumble Tart................................10
16.   Best Plum And Amaretti Crumble Recipe 10
17.   Blueberry Teacake With Crumble Topping 11
18.   Brilliant Apple Crumble 11
19.   Caramel And Pecan Apple Crumble..........12
20.   Chai Spiced Custard Apple Crumble Recipe 12
21.   Cinnamon And Pear Crumble Cake Recipe 13
22.   Coconut Apple Crumble..........................13
23.   Crumble Topping Recipe..........................14
24.   Crunchy Rhubarb Custard Recipe.............14
25.   Easy Apple Crumble Recipe......................14
26.   Easy Peach Crumble 15
27.   Fruit Mince Crumble Slice Recipe.............15
28.   Individual Apple Crumble 15
29.   Joanne's Easy Apple Crumble...................16
30.   Lemon Crumble 16
31.   Lemon And Lime Crumble Slice...............17
32.   Maggie's Apple Crumble 17
33.   Mixed Berries And Pecan Crumble Cake .17
34.   Mixed Up Dessert Recipe.........................18
35.   Mum's Fruit Crumble Recipe.....................18
36.   Muscat And Orange Glazed Peaches With Mascarpone And Crumbled Amaretti Recipe......18
37.   Nana Grace's Apple Crumble Recipe 19
38.   Paul's Hot Black Forest Crumble 19
39.   Peach Crumble 19
40.   Peach And Raspberry Crumble Recipe 20
41.   Plum Crumble 20
42.   Quick Rhubarb Crumble 21
43.   Rhubarb And Apple Crumble 21
44.   Rhubarb And Apple Crumble Recipe........21
45.   Scary Halloween Recipes.........................22
46.   Strawberry Crumble 22
47.   Sweet Berry Crumble 23
48.   Tania's Crumble 23
49.   Traditional German Apple Crumble Recipe 23
50.   Whole Apple Crumbles Recipe 24

INDEX **25**

CONCLUSION **26**

50 Awesome Crumble Recipes

***

1. 4 3 2 1 Crumble Topping

Serving: 4 | Prep: 15mins | Cook: 15mins | Ready in: 30mins

Ingredients

- 4 tbs plain flour
- 3 tbs coconut
- 2 tbs sugar
- 1 tbs butter

Direction

- Mix dry ingredients.
- Melt butter.
- Add to mixture.
- Sprinkle mixture onto fruit and bake at 180C until cooked.

2. Ange's Easy Tropical Pineapple Crumble Recipe

Serving: 8 | Prep: 40mins | Cook: 35mins | Ready in: 75mins

Ingredients

- 150g plain flour
- 100g almond meal
- 60g organic raw sugar
- 150g Nuttelex coconut margarine
- 12g vanilla sugar
- 1 pinch sea salt
- Filling
- 650g pineapple fresh cubed
- 1 tbs vanilla sugar
- 1/2 tsp Dutch cinnamon
- 25g organic raw sugar
- 1 tbs potato starch
- Crumble
- 100g plain flour
- 50g desiccated coconut
- 100g organic raw sugar
- 1 tbs raw sugar
- 1 tbs desiccated coconut

Direction

- For the base, add all ingredients into a bowl and mix with your hands well until you reach a smooth dough. Wrap in cling film and refrigerate until needed.
- To prepare the filling, start by cutting the pineapple and removing the skin and stump. Cut into small cubes and add into a bowl. Add the other ingredients, then mix well and set aside.
- Add all ingredients for the crumble into a bowl. Bring everything together with your fingers and crumble. Refrigerate.
- Preheat oven to 170C.
- Remove base dough from the fridge. Roll out with a rolling pin to about a 1cm thick base. Cover a spring form baking pan with baking paper. Add base carefully into the pan and use your hands to even and smooth the bottom and sides. Make the frame about 5cm high.
- Bake for 10 minutes and remove from the oven again.
- Add pineapple and push down the filling a bit. Even the top with a spoon.
- Mix the crumble with another tbs of raw sugar and coconut and then carefully top the filling with the crumble.
- Bake for 35 minutes. If the crumble is turning too dark, just move the cake to the lowest rack and bake until finished.

- Remove from the oven and allow to cool down.

3. Apple Crumble

Serving: 2 | Prep: 10mins | Cook: 30mins | Ready in: 40mins

Ingredients

- 2 apple cored cored peeled quartered
- 15 g butter
- 1/2 cup plain flour
- 1/4 cup brown sugar
- 1/4 cup coconut
- 1/2 tsp ground cinnamon

Direction

- Place apples into a small amount of boiling water in pot. Cook with lid on until tender.
- In a separate bowl, rub butter or margarine into flour, using fingertips, until mixture resembles breadcrumbs. Add brown sugar and coconut.
- Drain apples and place them into prepared ovenproof dish, sprinkle with cinnamon.
- Top with crumble mixture.
- Bake at 180C for 20 minutes.

4. Apple Crumble Cake

Serving: 8 | Prep: 15mins | Cook: 40mins | Ready in: 55mins

Ingredients

- 1 1/2 cups self-raising flour
- 1/2 cup caster sugar
- 115g butter
- 1 egg lightly beaten
- 440g canned pie apples sliced
- 1/4 cup icing sugar *to decorate

Direction

- Sift flour and sugar.
- Quickly break the butter into the dry mixture until it resembles crumbs.
- Add egg and gently mix through with a fork until it resembles crumbs.
- Press just under half the mixture into a greased and lined 20cm round tin.
- Top with apple.
- Sprinkle over remaining crumbs.
- Bake at 180C for 40 minutes. Cool on wire rack.
- Dust with icing sugar and a dollop of thickened cream to serve.

5. Apple Crumble Custard Hearts Recipe

Serving: 0 | Prep: 30mins | Cook: 15mins | Ready in: 45mins

Ingredients

- 2 apples coarsely chopped cored cored
- 2 tsp water
- 125 g butter softened
- 1/3 cup brown sugar
- 1 cup self-raising flour
- 3/4 cup plain flour
- 1/4 cup oat bran
- 1/4 cup desiccated coconut
- 1 tsp ground cinnamon
- 2 tbs apple juice concentrate
- 250 g Pauls custard
- 160 ml cream
- 1 tbs icing sugar

Direction

- Preheat oven 160 fan-forced. Line baking trays with baking paper.
- Stew apples with the water in a small saucepan, covered, until tender. Mash and cool. Reserve 1/3 of the stewed apple to serve.

- Beat butter, sugar and apple concentrate in a bowl with an electric mixer until combined.
- In two batches, stir in sifted flours, oat bran, 2/3 of the stewed apple, coconut and cinnamon.
- Knead dough on floured surface until smooth. Roll half the dough between two sheets of baking paper until 1cm thick. Roll the other half until 2cm thick. Refrigerate 30 minutes.
- Using a larger sized heart-shaped cookie cutter, cut 12 hearts from dough. Place shapes on oven tray.
- Bake biscuits about 12-15 minutes until slightly golden. Cool.
- Using a smaller heart shape cutter, cut out the centre of the 6 thicker (2 cm) cookies, then place on top of a full cookie.
- Fill each heart with custard. Dust with icing sugar and serve with cream or ice cream and remaining stewed apple.

6. Apple Crumble For Two

Serving: 2 | Prep: 10mins | Cook: 20mins | Ready in: 30mins

Ingredients

- 200 g canned pie apple chopped
- 1/2 tsp ground cinnamon
- Topping
- 1 Weet-Bix crushed
- 2 tbs natural muesli
- 2 tbs walnuts crushed
- 1 tbs brown sugar
- 1 tsp ground cinnamon
- 2 tbs butter melted

Direction

- Preheat oven to 180C (fan forced).
- Combine apple and cinnamon, and divide mixture across two single-serve oven dishes.
- Combine dry topping ingredients. Stir in butter.

- Spread over apple.
- Bake for 20 minutes until topping is golden.

7. Apple Crumble Recipe

Serving: 8 | Prep: 25mins | Cook: 85mins | Ready in: 110mins

Ingredients

- 6 Granny Smith apples large
- 2 tbs white sugar
- 2 tsp ground cinnamon
- Crust
- 115 g butter
- 2 tbs white sugar
- 1 egg
- 2 cups plain flour
- 1 tsp baking powder
- 1/4 cup custard powder
- Crumble
- 3/4 cup white sugar
- 3/4 cup butter
- 1 1/4 cups plain flour
- 1/3 cup shredded coconut
- 1/3 cup rolled oats

Direction

- Preheat the oven to 190C.
- To make the filling, boil the apples with enough water to cover. Reduce heat to low and simmer for 15 minutes.
- Drain the apples and allow to cool.
- Pour over sugar sprinkle the cinnamon powder onto the apples.
- To make the crust, in a bowl, whip together the butter and white sugar until fluffy and mix in the egg. In a separate bowl, mix the flour, baking powder and custard powder together.
- Mix into the butter mixture. Press it into the bottom and up the sides of a 22cm spring form pan.
- Pour the apples into the crust.

- To make the crumble, mix all the crumble ingredients together using your hands, until it resembles crumbs.
- Bake for 45 minutes to an hour or until golden brown.

8. Apple Crumble With Maple Syrup, Walnuts And Oats

Serving: 8 | Prep: 10mins | Cook: 50mins | Ready in: 60mins

Ingredients

- 8 apples peeled
- 1 1/4 cups maple syrup
- 1/2 tsp ground cinnamon
- 1/4 tsp nutmeg
- 1/2 cup toasted walnuts chopped
- 0.6 cup brown sugar
- 1 cup plain flour
- 1/2 cup rolled oats
- 6 tbs salted butter diced

Direction

- Preheat oven to 190C.
- Cut apple into 8 wedges each. Put apple wedges into dish and toss together with the maple syrup, the nutmeg and cinnamon.
- Scatter the walnuts over top.
- Stir together the brown sugar and flour, add butter and rub in, add oats.
- Sprinkle over apples.
- Bake for 45 to 50 minutes, or until the apples are tender and the topping is crisp.
- Serve with ice-cream, cream or custard.

9. Apple Crumble With White Choc Bits

Serving: 6 | Prep: 10mins | Cook: 20mins | Ready in: 30mins

Ingredients

- 800 g canned pie apple
- 1/4 cup plain flour
- 1 cup oats
- 1/2 cup brown sugar
- 1/2 cup walnuts
- 1 cup white chocolate chips
- 50 g butter chopped room temperature

Direction

- Preheat oven 180C (160C fan forced).
- Place pie apples into a medium sized baking dish.
- Combine flour, oats, sugar and nuts in a bowl.
- Add butter and, using fingertips, rub in until combined.
- Add chocolate bits and mix in.
- Sprinkle over apples.
- Bake for 15-20 minutes, until crumble is crisp.
- Serve with cream, ice-cream, yoghurt or custard.

10. Apple And Custard ANZAC Bickie Crumble Recipe

Serving: 4 | Prep: 15mins | Cook: 25mins | Ready in: 40mins

Ingredients

- 5 Granny Smith apples
- 1/4 tsp ground cinnamon
- 3 tbs sultanas
- 1 cup plain flour
- 1 cup desiccated coconut
- 1 cup rolled oats
- 50 g caster sugar

- 100 g brown sugar
- 120 g butter cubed
- 2 tbs golden syrup
- 1/2 tsp bicarbonate of soda
- 2 tbs water
- 2 cup Pauls thick vanilla custard

Direction

- Peel and core apples, cut into 1 cm thick slices. Toss with cinnamon and simmer in a saucepan over low heat until just soft, but still holding their shape (You can add a little water to saucepan to stop the apples sticking). Remove from heat and allow to cool while preparing the biscuit mixture.
- Mix flour, coconut, oats and sugar in a bowl.
- In a saucepan heat butter, golden syrup and water until the butter has melted. Add bicarbonate of soda and combine with the flour mixture. Allow to cool slightly.
- Place large spoonfuls the of apple mixture into a deep pie tin or heat proof dish, leave a little space between each spoonful, sprinkle with half the sultanas, fill the gaps with heaped spoonfuls of thick vanilla custard, add a second layer of apples, sultanas and a little custard (too much will bubble through the biscuit topping).
- Roll the Anzac biscuit mixture into small balls and flatten with a fork. Carefully lift biscuits with a spatula and arrange on top of the apple mixture.
- Bake at 160C (fan forced) for 15 minutes, or until the topping is golden, rotating the dish once during cooking to give even colour.

11. Appleberry Crumble

Serving: 6 | Prep: 20mins | Cook: 50mins | Ready in: 70mins

Ingredients

- Base

- 375 g sweet plain biscuits crushed
- 200 g butter melted
- Filling
- 5 apple cored cored peeled sliced
- 100 g caster sugar
- 1 lemon juiced zested
- 1 1/2 tbs rosewater essence optional
- 500 g mixed berries
- Topping
- 300 g plain flour
- 150 g butter cubed
- 150 g caster sugar
- 1/2 tsp ground cinnamon
- 2 tsp caster sugar

Direction

- Base: Mix melted butter and biscuit crumbs together.
- Press into the base and three quarters up the sides of a 28 cm spring form tin. Set aside.
- Filling: In a pan, place apples, caster sugar, lemon juice and zest and rose water essence and cook over a low heat until apples are soft.
- Layer apples and berries in prepared tin until they are level with the top of the biscuit base.
- Topping: Rub flour into butter until mixture resembles fine breadcrumbs. Stir through 150 g caster sugar.
- Place over the top of the apple and berries and sprinkle with combined cinnamon and 2 teaspoons of caster sugar.
- Bake at 180C for 30-40 minutes or until golden.
- Leave to cool before removing from the tin.
- Serve warm or cold with double thick cream, custard or ice-cream.

12. Banana Cake With Crumble Topping

Serving: 10 | Prep: 15mins | Cook: 45mins | Ready in: 60mins

Ingredients

- 1/3 cup olive oil
- 1 cup brown sugar
- 2 egg
- 3 banana mashed ripe
- 1/2 tsp vanilla extract
- 2 cup plain flour
- 3 tsp baking powder
- 1/2 tsp bicarbonate of soda
- 1 pinch salt
- 1/2 tsp ground cinnamon
- 1/2 cup milk
- Crumble Topping
- 35 g butter
- 3 tbs walnuts chopped
- 3 tbs brown sugar
- 3 tbs plain flour
- 1/2 tsp baking powder
- 1 tsp ground cinnamon

Direction

- Crumble: Mix butter into the dry ingredients until well combined. Put to one side.
- Grease a 20 cm spring form tin and preheat oven to 180C.
- Combine olive oil and sugar in a large bowl and beat in eggs one at a time.
- Add bananas and vanilla extract.
- Sift dry ingredients and add to the mixture in two batches, alternating with the milk. Spoon the mixture into the tin.
- Sprinkle the crumble topping mix over the cake batter, pressing it in lightly before baking.
- Bake cake for 45 minutes. Allow to cool before removing from the tin.

13. Banana Crumble

Serving: 4 | Prep: 15mins | Cook: 30mins | Ready in: 45mins

Ingredients

- 5 banana
- 1 tbs lemon juice
- 150 g butter
- 150 g soft brown sugar
- 3 cup rolled oats
- 30 g walnuts chopped

Direction

- Slice the bananas into a casserole dish.
- Sprinkle the lemon juice over the bananas.
- Melt the butter and sugar together.
- Add the rolled oats, walnuts and cinnamon to the butter and sugar mixture, and combine.
- Place mixture over the bananas.
- Bake at 180C for 20 minutes.

14. Banana And Pear Crumble

Serving: 2 | Prep: 15mins | Cook: 35mins | Ready in: 50mins

Ingredients

- 3 pear
- 2 banana
- 100 g cooking chocolate
- 100 g plain flour
- 50 g caster sugar
- 100 g butter

Direction

- Preheat oven to 200C (180C fan-forced).
- Peel and core pears, cut into cubes. Peel and slice the bananas. Place the fruit in an oven proof dish.
- Cut chocolate into pieces and scatter over the fruit.
- Combine the flour and butter to resemble breadcrumbs, add the sugar, mix and spread over the top of the fruit.
- Bake for 25 minutes until topping is golden.
- Serve with vanilla ice-cream or creme fraiche.

15. Berry Crumble Tart

Serving: 0 | Prep: 5mins | Cook: 30mins | Ready in: 35mins

Ingredients

- 2 cup thick vanilla custard
- 2 cup almond meal
- 400 g frozen mixed berries
- 2 tbs icing sugar
- 4 sheets shortcrust pastry cut in half thawed
- Crumble
- 1 cup rolled oats
- 300 g plain flour
- 200 g butter
- 100 g caster sugar

Direction

- Preheat oven to 170C.
- Line 1 pastry half into each pie mold and cut off overhang.
- Mix custard and almond meal. Spoon 1 tablespoon of mixture into each pie base.
- Sprinkle mixed berries on top, spreading evenly between pies.
- To make crumble: Mix all crumble ingredients together with your fingertips until combined
- Sprinkle 1 cup of the crumble evenly over the 4 pies.
- Dust pies with icing sugar and serve with more thick vanilla custard.
- Bake the pies for 25-35 minutes.

16. Best Plum And Amaretti Crumble Recipe

Serving: 6 | Prep: 10mins | Cook: 90mins | Ready in: 100mins

Ingredients

- 12 plum halved just ripe pitted
- 1/3 cup caster sugar
- 1 tbs lemon juice
- 2 tbs water
- 2 star anise
- 1 cinnamon stick
- Crumble
- 2 tbs plain flour
- 1/4 tsp ground cinnamon
- 20 g butter chilled diced
- 1 tbs brown sugar
- 6 amaretti biscuits lightly crushed
- Mascarpone Custard
- 250 g mascarpone
- 1 cup Pauls Double Thick French Vanilla Custard
- 1/4 cup icing sugar sifted

Direction

- Preheat oven to 180°C.
- Place plums cut side down with sugar, lemon juice and water in a baking dish and stir to combine. Allow to stand for 10 minutes.
- Place star anise and cinnamon with plums and cover dish with foil.
- Bake for 35 minutes or until plums are tender and just starting to collapse.
- Use a slotted spoon to transfer plums to a bowl. Place liquid along with star anise and cinnamon in a small saucepan and simmer 2 minutes or until syrupy, then pour over plums.
- Cool, then cover and refrigerate until ready to use.
- To make crumble, combine flour and cinnamon in a bowl.
- Add butter and rub into flour with your fingertips until the mixture resembles coarse breadcrumbs. Add the sugar and stir to combine.
- Spread onto an oven tray lined with baking paper. Bake for 15 minutes, or until golden brown, checking occasionally to ensure evenly cooked.
- Cool, then add crushed amaretti biscuits and stir to combine. Store in an airtight container.

- To make mascarpone custard, place mascarpone into a bowl and beat with a wooden spoon until smooth.
- Add custard and icing sugar and beat to combine. Divide plums and juice between 6 glasses. Top with mascarpone cream and sprinkle with crumble.
- Divide plums and juice between 6 glasses. Top with mascarpone cream and sprinkle with crumble.

17. Blueberry Teacake With Crumble Topping

Serving: 0 | Prep: 10mins | Cook: 50mins | Ready in: 60mins

Ingredients

- 60 g soft butter
- 2/3 cup sugar
- 1/2 tsp vanilla essence
- 1 egg
- 2 cup plain flour
- 2 tsp baking powder
- 1/4 tsp salt
- 1/2 cup milk
- 1 1/2 cup fresh blueberries
- Crumble topping
- 1/4 cup brown sugar
- 1/4 cup plain flour
- 1/2 tsp ground cinnamon
- 50 g butter

Direction

- Cream butter and sugar, then beat in vanilla essence and egg.
- Sift flour, baking powder and salt together.
- Stir butter mixture into the dry ingredients along with milk, without over-mixing.
- Fold in the blueberries. The mixture will be quite stiff, add extra milk if too dry.
- Spread cake mixture into a greased and lined 20 x 20 cm cake tin.

- Crumble: Chop or grate butter into the dry ingredients and combine.
- Sprinkle topping over the cake mixture.
- Bake at 180C for 40-50 minutes.

18. Brilliant Apple Crumble

Serving: 6 | Prep: 30mins | Cook: 60mins | Ready in: 90mins

Ingredients

- 5 apple firm
- 3 tbs sugar
- 1 cinnamon stick medium
- 2 tbs water
- 225 g plain flour
- 115 g unsalted butter cubed
- 100 g white sugar

Direction

- Preheat the oven to 180C.
- Peel, core and slice apples into thick slices.
- Place into pan and add sugar or sweetener.
- Add water and cinnamon stick and cook, covered, for approximately 10 minutes until apples are soft when tested with a fork. Don't over cook, the apples should keep their shape. Set aside.
- Place the flour into a bowl and add the butter. Crumble the flour and butter using fingertips, rubbing together lightly. Keep hands high.
- Stir in the sugar.
- Place the cooked apple mixture into a medium size heat proof dish.
- Carefully add the crumble mixture on top, making sure all the apple mixture is covered.
- Bake at 180C for 30 minutes. Apples should be bubbling and the topping just turning colour.
- Serve with cream, ice-cream or custard.

19. Caramel And Pecan Apple Crumble

Serving: 6 | Prep: 30mins | Cook: 35mins | Ready in: 65mins

Ingredients

- 8 granny smith apple
- 1 tbs brown sugar
- 1 tsp ground cinnamon
- Caramel sauce
- 85 g unsalted butter
- 1/2 cup thickened cream
- 1/2 cup brown sugar
- 2 tbs pecans chopped
- Crumbled topping
- 200 g unsalted butter melted
- 1 1/4 cup plain flour
- 1 cup rolled oats
- 3/4 cup caster sugar
- 1/2 tsp ground cinnamon
- 2 tbs pecans chopped

Direction

- Peel, core and quarter the apples. Place in a saucepan along with the brown sugar and cinnamon. Simmer over medium high heat stirring for approx 15 mins or until the apples are still firm but tender.
- Set the apples aside and in the same saucepan add the cream, butter and brown sugar to make the caramel sauce. Over a medium heat, stir until the butter and sugar have melted and the sauce has begun to simmer. Allow the sauce to simmer for 2 mins before adding the apples and chopped pecans back into the saucepan. Fold the apples through the sauce and pour into a small baking dish (a 20cm dish is perfect).
- Preheat the oven to 180C degrees.
- Prepare the crumble topping - Melt the butter in the microwave. Add the flour, sugar, oats ,cinnamon and chopped nuts. Mix well and crumble evenly over the prepared apples.

- Bake in preheated oven for 35 mins or until browned. Enjoy.

20. Chai Spiced Custard Apple Crumble Recipe

Serving: 8 | Prep: 30mins | Cook: 40mins | Ready in: 70mins

Ingredients

- Crumble
- 220 g unsalted butter
- 1/3 cup white sugar
- 1 tsp vanilla essence
- 2 cups plain flour
- 1 egg
- 1/2 cup rolled oats
- 1 tbs sliced almonds
- 2 tsp chai spice mix
- Custard apples
- 1 custard apple large
- 1 tbs lemon juice
- 1/2 cup white sugar
- 20 g unsalted butter
- 2 tbs plain flour
- Filling
- 1 tbs honey
- 100 g cream cheese
- 200 g Greek yoghurt
- 1 egg

Direction

- Preheat oven to 180C.
- Grease a 25cm x 15cm casserole dish, and set aside.
- Custard apples: Cut your custard apple into quarters, scoop out the seeds, cut off the skin and dice the flesh.
- Place your diced custard apple, 1tbs lemon juice, 1/2 cup granulated sugar, 20g butter and 2tbs plain flour into a saucepan over medium heat.

- Stir gently until the sugar has melted and the sauce has thickened. Remove from the heat and set aside to cool slightly.
- Filling: In a large mixing bowl, combine 1tbs honey, 1 egg, 200g Greek style yoghurt and 100g cream cheese with electric beaters until well combined and smooth.
- Pour your custard apples into your yoghurt mix, and combine gently with a spatula.
- Pour into your pre-prepared casserole dish, use your spatula to ensure your custard apples are spread through the mix evenly, and set aside.
- Crumble: Combine 220g unsalted butter, 2 cups plain flour, 2tsp chai spice mix, 1/3 cup granulated sugar and 1tsp vanilla extract in a food processor. Blitz for a couple of seconds to combine.
- Add 1 egg to the food processor, blitz until well combined.
- Then add in your 1/2 cup rolled oats and 1tbsp almonds and blitz on low for roughly 10 seconds to chop them roughly.
- Sprinkle your crumble evenly across the top of your custard apple mix, and place in the oven to bake for roughly 40 minutes, or until the top of your crumble is golden.

21. Cinnamon And Pear Crumble Cake Recipe

Serving: 8 | Prep: 20mins | Cook: 70mins | Ready in: 90mins

Ingredients

- 125g butter chopped softened
- 3/4 cup caster sugar
- 1 tsp vanilla extract
- 2 eggs
- 1 cup plain flour sifted
- 1 tsp baking powder
- 1 tsp ground cinnamon
- 1 1/2 tbs almond meal
- 1/2 cup milk
- 2 pears chopped cored peeled
- Crumble Topping
- 1/2 cup plain flour
- 1 1/2 tbs brown sugar
- 1/4 tsp baking powder
- 60g butter chopped softened

Direction

- Preheat oven to 160C.
- Beat butter, sugar and vanilla with electric mixer until pale and creamy.
- Gradually add the eggs and beat well.
- Add the flour, baking powder, cinnamon and almond meal, and beat to combine.
- Fold through the milk and pears.
- To make the topping, combine flour, sugar and baking powder in a bowl.
- Add the butter rub it into the flour mixture with fingertips.
- Line the base of a lightly greased round spring-form cake tin with baking paper.
- Spoon in cake mixture and top with crumble.
- Bake for 1 hour and 10 minutes or until cooked when tested with a skewer.
- Allow to cool in the tin.

22. Coconut Apple Crumble

Serving: 2 | Prep: 10mins | Cook: 30mins | Ready in: 40mins

Ingredients

- 1 pink lady apple finely sliced
- 1/3 cup frozen blueberries
- 1/2 cup rolled oats
- 1 tbs plain flour
- 1 tbs butter
- 1/4 cup macadamias chopped
- 1/3 cup coconut shredded
- 1 tbs brown sugar
- 2 tbs water

Direction

- Preheat oven to 180C.
- Lay the sliced apples into each ramekin. Top with blueberries and add 1 tablespoon of water into each dish.
- Add the remaining ingredients into a bowl and rub the mixture with your hands to combine the butter throughout.
- Add the crumble mix to the top of the apples and place into the oven. Cook for 20-30 minutes or until golden. Serve with your favourite ice cream.

23. Crumble Topping Recipe

Serving: 10 | Prep: 15mins | Cook: 40mins | Ready in: 55mins

Ingredients

- 1/2 cup plain flour
- 1/2 cup rolled oats
- 1/4 cup brown sugar firmly packed
- 1/3 cup desiccated coconut
- 1/2 tsp ground cinnamon
- 90g butter chopped

Direction

- Mix to combine flour, oats, sugar, coconut and cinnamon.
- Rub in butter with fingertips until mix resembles coarse breadcrumbs.
- Sprinkle topping over stewed fruit.
- Bake at 180C for 25-30 minutes.

24. Crunchy Rhubarb Custard Recipe

Serving: 6 | Prep: 15mins | Cook: 25mins | Ready in: 40mins

Ingredients

- 3 cup rhubarb cooked
- 90g butter
- 1/2 cup plain flour
- 1/4 cup coconut
- 2 tbs brown sugar
- 3/4 cup rolled oats
- 1/4 cup flaked almonds
- 1/2 tsp ground cinnamon
- 2 tbs custard powder
- 2 cup milk
- 1/3 cup sugar

Direction

- Spread drained rhubarb over the base of an ovenproof dish.
- Combine custard powder, milk and sugar in a small saucepan and heat gently to make custard.
- Pour custard over rhubarb.
- Melt butter, add brown sugar, flour, coconut, rolled oats and cinnamon.
- Sprinkle roughly over custard.
- Bake at 150C until topping is golden brown and crunchy.
- Serve warm with whipped cream.

25. Easy Apple Crumble Recipe

Serving: 4 | Prep: 15mins | Cook: 35mins | Ready in: 50mins

Ingredients

- 8 apple
- 3 tbs brown sugar
- 2 cup basic muesli
- 4 tbs butter melted
- 2 tbs water
- 1 tsp ground cinnamon *to taste

Direction

- Peel and core apples, add 1 tablespoon of brown sugar, cinnamon and some of the water. Stew until tender.
- Melt the butter and add to the muesli with a small amount of cinnamon and the remaining brown sugar. Mix until combined.
- Place apples in baking dish and top with the crumble mix.
- Bake at 180C until crumble is golden brown.
- Serve with custard, cream or ice-cream.

26. Easy Peach Crumble

Serving: 6 | Prep: 10mins | Cook: 20mins | Ready in: 30mins

Ingredients

- 1/2 cup plain flour
- 1/2 cup butter cold
- 1/2 cup custard powder
- 1/2 cup sugar
- 2 kg peach cooked peeled

Direction

- Drain any liquid from the cooked fruit, and place fruit in a large oven proof dish.
- Sift together the flour and custard powder, add the sugar.
- Rub in the butter with fingertips until no large lumps remain.
- Place mixture over the fruit. If you have more fruit, or a wide dish, use ¾ cup of all ingredients.
- Bake at 180C for 20 minutes.
- Serve warm with ice-cream.

27. Fruit Mince Crumble Slice Recipe

Serving: 0 | Prep: 15mins | Cook: 35mins | Ready in: 50mins

Ingredients

- 2 cup fruit mince *see notes
- 250 g butter
- 1 cup brown sugar
- 1 egg
- 1 tsp vanilla extract
- 2 1/2 cup plain flour
- 2 cup rolled oats

Direction

- Preheat oven to 160C. Line a slice pan (18cmx28cm) with baking paper.
- Beat butter and sugar with an electric mixer until pale and creamy. Add in the vanilla and egg. Stir in flour and rolled oats until combined.
- Place half the mixture into the tin and press down firmly. Top with the fruit mince and crumble the remaining mixture over the top, pressing down gently. Bake for 35minutes.

28. Individual Apple Crumble

Serving: 1 | Prep: 10mins | Cook: 15mins | Ready in: 25mins

Ingredients

- 1 granny smith apple large
- 1/4 cup water
- 1 tbs plain flour
- 1 tbs brown sugar
- 1 tsp butter

Direction

- Preheat oven to 180C degrees (160C degrees fan-forced). Cut the apple into thin slices and place into the ramekin with the water. Microwave on high for 2 minute or until apples are soft.

- In a small bowl add the flour, butter and sugar. With your hands rub the ingredients together until it changes to a crumbly texture. Sprinkle the mixture on top of the apples.
- Place the ramekin in the oven for 10 minutes or until the crumble looks golden and delicious. Serve with a bit of dollop/heavy cream and devour your scrumptious dessert!

29. Joanne's Easy Apple Crumble

Serving: 6 | Prep: 15mins | Cook: 35mins | Ready in: 50mins

Ingredients

- 6 apple cored cored peeled
- 2 tsp ground cinnamon
- 1/4 cup brown sugar
- 1 cup self-raising flour sifted
- 1 cup oats
- 1/2 cup brown sugar
- 1/2 cup coconut
- 3 tbs butter

Direction

- Place apples, cinnamon and ¼ cup of brown sugar in a saucepan.
- Cover with water, bring slowly to the boil, stirring occasionally. Drain.
- Place the rest of the dry ingredients into a bowl and mix.
- Rub in enough butter until mix feels slightly wet, or sticks when squeezed.
- Place cooked apples into a greased casserole dish, cover with crumble mix and press down slightly.
- Bake at 180C, uncovered, for 20 minutes or until golden brown on top.
- Serve hot or cold with ice-cream, custard or cream.

30. Lemon Crumble

Serving: 6 | Prep: 10mins | Cook: 35mins | Ready in: 45mins

Ingredients

- 125g butter
- 125g sugar
- 125g self-raising flour
- 1 1/2 cups coconut
- Filling
- 125g sugar
- 3 tbs cornflour
- 1/2 tsp salt
- 2 cups milk
- 1 tsp lemon rind grated
- 1/2 cup lemon juice
- 2 tbs butter
- 2 eggs lightly beaten

Direction

- Crumble: Rub together all crumble ingredients.
- Press half into a pie plate.
- Filling: Blend cornflour, sugar and salt with a little milk.
- Heat remaining milk, then add to the cornflour mixture to make a custard, then cook until it thickens.
- Add rind, juice, butter and lastly lightly beaten eggs.
- Pour onto crumb crust and then sprinkle remaining half of crumble on top of the mixture.
- Bake 20 minutes at 180C or until set.

31. Lemon And Lime Crumble Slice

Serving: 4 | Prep: 10mins | Cook: 45mins | Ready in: 55mins

Ingredients

- Base
- 150 g unsalted butter
- 1/2 tsp vanilla extract
- 1/3 cup caster sugar
- 1 tbs cornflour
- 1 1/3 cup gluten-free plain flour
- Lemon topping
- 4 egg
- 2 lemon juiced zested
- 1/3 cup lime juice
- 1/3 cup gluten-free plain flour
- 1 cup caster sugar

Direction

- Base: Melt butter in microwave.
- Stir vanilla and sugar into butter mixture until well combined.
- Sift flour over butter mixture and, using a wooden spoon, stir to combine into a sticky dough.
- Press into a lined and greased baking tray and bake for 15 minutes on 180C.
- Set aside to cool.
- Topping: Whisk eggs, lemon rind, flour and sugar together until well combined.
- Whisk in lemon and lime juice.
- Pour over base and bake for 20-25 minutes at 180C.
- Remove from oven, cut to desired sized slices and leave to cool in tray.

32. Maggie's Apple Crumble

Serving: 6 | Prep: 15mins | Cook: 20mins | Ready in: 35mins

Ingredients

- 1 cup sugar
- 1 cup desiccated coconut
- 1 cup self-raising flour
- 1 tbs butter
- 6 apple peeled sliced

Direction

- Preheat oven to 180C.
- Stew the apples in a little water until soft. Pour into a pie dish.
- Cream sugar and butter.
- Add self-raising flour and coconut to the sugar and butter mixture.
- Sprinkle evenly over apples.
- Bake for approximately 20 minutes or until crumble is golden brown.

33. Mixed Berries And Pecan Crumble Cake

Serving: 0 | Prep: 10mins | Cook: 55mins | Ready in: 65mins

Ingredients

- 1 1/4 cup plain flour
- 1 tsp bicarbonate of soda
- 1 tsp ground cinnamon
- 3/4 cup caster sugar
- 3/4 cup olive oil
- 300 g mixed berries
- 2 egg lightly beaten
- 1 tsp vanilla essence
- Crumble
- 1/2 cup plain flour
- 60 g butter chopped
- 1 tsp ground cinnamon
- 1/4 cup brown sugar
- 1/3 cup pecans chopped

Direction

- Preheat oven to 180C. Lightly grease and fully line a 20 cm ring or bundt pan.

- Sift flour, bicarbonate of soda and cinnamon into a large bowl, stir in sugar.
- In a separate bowl whisk together oil, eggs and vanilla.
- Blend into flour mixture, stir until combined. Mix in the berries and pecan nuts. Spoon mixture into pan and smooth the top.
- Crumble: Place flour, butter, cinnamon, sugar into a processor, process until combined. Add nuts, Sprinkle over cake mixture.
- Bake for 50-55 minutes or until cooked. Stand cake for 10 minutes. Turn onto wire rack with the crumble side up.

34. Mixed Up Dessert Recipe

Serving: 6 | Prep: 15mins | Cook: 45mins | Ready in: 60mins

Ingredients

- 440 g canned fruit salad
- 450 g (crushed) canned pineapple drained
- 1/2 cup brown sugar
- 470 g vanilla cake mix
- 1/2 cup desiccated coconut
- 1/2 cup mixed nuts chopped
- 1/2 cup butter melted

Direction

- Layer ingredients in deep casserole dish in order mentioned.
- Sprinkle over butter.
- Bake for approximately 40 minutes at 180C until golden brown.

35. Mum's Fruit Crumble Recipe

Serving: 2 | Prep: 10mins | Cook: 25mins | Ready in: 35mins

Ingredients

- 1/3 cup plain flour
- 1/3 cup sugar
- 1 tsp cinnamon
- 30 g butter
- 2 cooking apples sliced
- 4 tbs water
- 1/3 cup oats *optional
- 1/3 cup desiccated coconut *optional
- 1/3 cup almonds sliced *optional

Direction

- Preheat oven to 180C.
- Combine all dry ingredients in a mixing bowl and then rub butter through it with your fingertips to create the crumble.
- In a small baking dish, add 4 tbs water. Layer sliced apples on top of water in the dish.
- Spread crumble evenly across the top of the apples.
- Bake for 25 minutes, or until crumble topping is golden.
- Serve with cream and ice cream.

36. Muscat And Orange Glazed Peaches With Mascarpone And Crumbled Amaretti Recipe

Serving: 4 | Prep: 45mins | Cook: 0S | Ready in: 45mins

Ingredients

- 250 ml muscat
- 160 ml fresh orange juice
- 80 g caster sugar
- 4 peaches firm halved
- 2 tbs mascarpone
- 4 amaretti biscuits crumbled

Direction

- Pour Muscat, orange juice and sugar into a deep frypan and bring to the boil over a medium to high heat. Cook for 3-5 minutes until reduced to a glaze thickness.

- Add peaches to frypan and cook for 2-4 minutes, stirring gently occasionally, until tender.
- Remove peaches with a holed spoon and place on serving plates. Keep warm.
- Simmer the glaze for 1-2 minutes until sticky.
- Drizzle over the peaches.
- Crumble amaretti over peaches and serve with mascarpone.

37. Nana Grace's Apple Crumble Recipe

Serving: 12 | Prep: 10mins | Cook: 30mins | Ready in: 40mins

Ingredients

- 90 g butter softened
- 1 cup self-raising flour
- 1/2 cup brown sugar
- 2 tsp ground cinnamon
- 1/2 cup desiccated coconut
- 800 g SPC tinned apple pie

Direction

- Pre-heat oven to 180 degrees and coat baking dish in cooking spray. Cover base of dish with apple. OPTIONAL: cook in microwave for 3 minutes or until apple is warm to help speed cooking time in oven.
- Rub butter and flour until it resembles bread crumbs.
- Add rest of ingredients (aside from apple) and mix. Cover apple with crumb mix and bake in oven for 30 minutes or until crumb is golden brown.
- Serve with custard and vanilla ice cream or cream.

38. Paul's Hot Black Forest Crumble

Serving: 8 | Prep: 10mins | Cook: 40mins | Ready in: 50mins

Ingredients

- 500 g cherries pitted
- 900 g chocolate custard
- 1/2 cup plain flour
- 1/2 cup rolled oats
- 1/4 cup brown sugar
- 1/3 cup chocolate custard powder
- 1/2 cup dark chocolate chips
- 90 g butter room temperature

Direction

- Preheat oven to 175C degrees.
- In a medium-sized oven proof dish, layer fresh pitted cherries and chocolate custard.
- Mix all dry ingredients, except choc chips, in a mixing bowl.
- Rub butter into dry ingredients until the mixture resembles breadcrumbs.
- Sprinkle crumble mixture over cherries and custard. Top with dark choc chips.
- Bake in oven for 35-40 minutes, until top is lightly browned and crusty and custard is bubbling.
- Serve hot or cold with cream or ice cream.

39. Peach Crumble

Serving: 3 | Prep: 15mins | Cook: 40mins | Ready in: 55mins

Ingredients

- 400 g (pie) canned peaches
- 1/2 cup plain flour
- 1/2 cup rolled oats
- 1/2 cup coconut
- 1/2 cup brown sugar

- 1/4 cup ground almonds
- 1/4 tsp vanilla essence
- 1/2 tsp ground cinnamon
- 1/2 tsp ground ginger
- 90 g butter chopped

Direction

- Place peaches evenly in the base of a small casserole dish.
- In a separate bowl, mix dry ingredients and spices together.
- Rub in butter until the mixture resembles coarse breadcrumbs. The mixture should just hold together when squeezed, but fall apart readily when dropped back in the bowl.
- Pile crumble topping over the fruit and bake at 180C for 40 minutes or until golden on top.

40. Peach And Raspberry Crumble Recipe

Serving: 1 | Prep: 10mins | Cook: 20mins | Ready in: 30mins

Ingredients

- 1 peach cut into 2cm pieces
- 1/4 cup fresh raspberries
- 1/2 tsp vanilla extract
- 1/4 tsp ground cinnamon
- 1 pinch sea salt
- 2 tbs rolled oats
- 1 1/2 tbs almonds raw roughly chopped unsalted
- 1/2 tbs chia seeds
- 2 tbs coconut flakes
- 1 tbs butter melted
- 1 1/2 tbs Greek yoghurt *to serve

Direction

- Preheat a fan-forced oven to 180C and lightly grease a small baking dish.

- Place the peaches and raspberries in the baking dish. Drizzle over vanilla extract and sprinkle over cinnamon and salt. Toss with your hands to coat the fruit.
- Evenly sprinkle over the oats, almonds, chia seeds and coconut flakes and drizzle over butter. Place into the oven to bake for 20 minutes until the top is crispy and golden.
- Serve with a dollop of yoghurt.

41. Plum Crumble

Serving: 2 | Prep: 15mins | Cook: 95mins | Ready in: 110mins

Ingredients

- 15 plum chopped peeled ripe
- 1/4 cup sugar
- 2 tbs water
- 1/2 cup brown sugar
- 1/4 cup self-raising flour
- 1/2 cup plain flour loosely packed
- 3 tbs margarine

Direction

- Preheat oven to 200C.
- Place plums into a medium sized saucepan. Add sugar and bring to the boil. If plums begin to stick or do not have enough juice, add water gradually.
- Boil for 30-60 minutes until sauce thickens. Cool.
- Combine both flours and brown sugar in a small mixing bowl. Add margarine and rub until mixture resembles crumble.
- Place the plums in a small casserole dish.
- Sprinkle crumble mixture over top, reduce oven temperature to 170-180C and bake for 20-25 minutes.

42. Quick Rhubarb Crumble

Serving: 4 | Prep: 15mins | Cook: 45mins | Ready in: 60mins

Ingredients

- 500 g rhubarb broken into chunks
- 1/2 cup sugar
- 1 tbs orange grated zested
- 1 pinch salt
- Crumble
- 1/2 cup brown sugar
- 1/2 cup rolled oats
- 1/2 cup self-raising flour
- 85 g butter diced

Direction

- Combine rhubarb, sugar, orange zest and salt in a greased casserole dish.
- Process sugar, flour and butter until crumbly. Add oats and just pulse to combine, so that some texture is retained.
- Spread over the rhubarb and bake at 180C for 40 minutes, or until fruit is tender and top is lightly browned.
- Serve with whipped cream, ice cream or custard.

43. Rhubarb And Apple Crumble

Serving: 6 | Prep: 15mins | Cook: 60mins | Ready in: 75mins

Ingredients

- 1 bunch rhubarb cut into pieces
- 5 green apple peeled
- 30 g sugar
- 1 tbs butter
- 1 tbs vanilla extract
- 1 tbs cornflour
- 1 tsp ginger grated
- 1 orange grated zested

- 1/2 orange juiced
- Topping
- 1 1/3 cup plain flour
- 1 tsp baking powder
- 100 g unsalted butter diced
- 3 tbs sugar
- 1 tbs brown sugar

Direction

- Preheat oven to 190C.
- Combine rhubard, apples, butter, vanilla, cornflour, ginger, juice and zest in a saucepan.
- Cook for about 5 minutes until the the rhubarb is slightly soft.
- Pour into ovenproof dish.
- Combine flour and baking powder in a bowl and rub in the butter using fingers, until mixture resembles breadcrumbs. Quickly mix in the sugars.
- Scatter topping over the fruit.
- Bake for 35-45 minutes until golden brown.

44. Rhubarb And Apple Crumble Recipe

Serving: 6 | Prep: 15mins | Cook: 50mins | Ready in: 65mins

Ingredients

- 15 stalks rhubarb
- 4 apple
- 1/2 cup sugar
- 1 tbs water
- Crumble topping
- 1/4 cup butter melted
- 1/3 cup brown sugar
- 2/3 cup oats
- 2/3 cup plain flour

Direction

- String rhubarb and cut into pieces 3 cm long.
- Peel, core and slice apples.

- Place fruit into a microwave container.
- Add sugar and a splash of water and cook on high for 10 minutes.
- Spoon fruit into a 2 L baking dish.
- Crumble topping: Place all ingredients into a bowl and mix well.
- Sprinkle topping over fruit and pat down firmly.
- Bake in a moderate oven for 25 minutes.
- Serve with ice-cream, cream or custard.

45. Scary Halloween Recipes

Serving: 2 | Prep: 20mins | Cook: 20mins | Ready in: 40mins

Ingredients

- 2 Modi apples cored peeled
- 2 tbs cane sugar
- 1 glass water
- 1 splash lemon juice
- 160 g fresh whipping cream
- 2 gelatine leaves
- 1 pinch icing sugar *to taste
- To decorate
- 1 handful cocoa shortbread cookies
- 4 sugar ghosts
- 4 cat tongue-type cookies
- 1 tube red gel icing

Direction

- Prepare the mousse: dice the apples, put them in a small pan with the cane sugar, the water and a splash of lemon juice.
- Cook until the apples are soft and the water has been absorbed.
- In the meantime, soak the gelatine in cold water for 5-8 minutes.
- Use a hand-held liquidiser to make a puree with the cooked apples.
- Squeeze the gelatine of excess water and add it to the hot apple puree to let it thaw.

- Whisk the whipping cream and sweeten it with the desired amount of icing sugar.
- Gradually add the whipped cream to the now cold apple puree.
- Pour the mixture into the pots and place them in the fridge for a few hours.
- Decorate and serve: crumble the cocoa shortbread cookies coarsely; write the acronym R.I.P. (Rest In Peace) on the cat tongues using the red gel.
- Spread the cookie "soil" over the apple mousse, put a cat tongue and a ghost in each pot. Happy Halloween!

46. Strawberry Crumble

Serving: 10 | Prep: 15mins | Cook: 60mins | Ready in: 75mins

Ingredients

- 500 g fresh strawberries halved
- 2 pear peeled thickly sliced
- 250 g frozen blueberries thawed
- 1 orange finely grated juiced
- 1 cup plain flour sifted
- 125 g butter chilled diced
- 1/2 cup brown sugar
- 1/2 cup toasted muesli

Direction

- Preheat oven to 180C.
- Fold strawberries, pears, berries, orange rind and juice together in a bowl.
- Spoon mixture into an oval pie dish or shallow ovenproof bowl.
- For the topping, rub butter into flour until it resembles breadcrumbs.
- Stir in sugar and muesli.
- Sprinkle topping over the fruit, covering completely.
- Bake for 30-40 minutes or until fruit is bubbling hot and topping is golden.
- Serve with whipped cream or custard.

47. Sweet Berry Crumble

Serving: 3 | Prep: 20mins | Cook: 20mins | Ready in: 40mins

Ingredients

- 60 g unsalted butter chopped
- 1/2 cup plain flour
- 3/4 cup rolled oats
- 3/4 cup brown sugar
- 1/2 cup desiccated coconut
- Fruit
- 1 cup fresh strawberries sliced
- 1 cup fresh raspberries whole
- 1 cup frozen blueberry
- 1 cup passionfruit pulp seeds removed

Direction

- Layer fruit in a 6-8 cup square casserole dish.
- Place dry ingredients into a large mixing bowl, rub in butter using fingertips, until well mixed.
- Sprinkle crumble mix over fruit.
- Bake in preheated oven at 150C fan-forced until golden brown, approximately 15 minutes.

48. Tania's Crumble

Serving: 4 | Prep: 10mins | Cook: 35mins | Ready in: 45mins

Ingredients

- 3 cup granny smith apple broken into chunks cored cored peeled
- 3/4 cup plain flour
- 1/2 cup sugar
- 1 cup pecans chopped
- 1/2 cup brown sugar tightly packed

- 1 cup rolled oats
- 1 tsp ground cinnamon
- 1 tsp ground nutmeg
- 1 tsp ground ginger
- 100 g butter melted

Direction

- Toss the apples, flour and sugar together to coat.
- Arrange the apples over the bottom of a baking dish. Discard the remaining flour and sugar mixture.
- Mix together pecans, brown sugar, oats, cinnamon, nutmeg and ginger.
- Add melted butter to the dry mixture and mix well.
- Cover apples with the nut mixture and bake at 180c for about 35 minutes or until bubbly and brown on top.
- Serve with ice cream.

49. Traditional German Apple Crumble Recipe

Serving: 0 | Prep: 45mins | Cook: 30mins | Ready in: 75mins

Ingredients

- 300g plain 00 flour
- 100g raw sugar organic
- 200g Nuttelex margarine
- 50ml almond milk
- 1 tbs vanilla sugar
- 1 tbs vanilla essence
- Filling
- 4 apples peeled cut into small pieces
- 3 tbs raw sugar
- 1 tbs vanilla sugar
- 1/2 lemon juiced
- 1 tsp Dutch cinnamon ground
- 1/4 cup raisins
- Crumble
- 100g plain 00 flour

- 100g raw sugar
- 80g Nuttelex margarine

Direction

- Preheat the oven to 180°C.
- Peel and cut the apples into small cubes. Mix with the lemon juice, sugar, vanilla sugar, raisins and cinnamon, then add to a medium saucepan. Cook for about 10 minutes then set aside to cool.
- Add all ingredients for the short crust pastry into a bowl and mix well. Tip the dough onto a floured surface and work into a smooth dough. Wrap with cling wrap and refrigerate for 30 minutes.
- Spray a spring form cake tin with some oil. Add the dough and spread across the bottom and 3/4 of the way up the side of the tin.
- Add all the ingredients for the crumble into a bowl. Pinch between your fingers until it forms a crumble texture. Put into the fridge until needed.
- Add the apples into the tin. Top with crumble. Place into a preheated oven and bake for 30 minutes. Remove from the oven and allow to cool down, then sprinkle with icing sugar. Enjoy.

50. Whole Apple Crumbles Recipe

Serving: 8 | Prep: 30mins | Cook: 20mins | Ready in: 50mins

Ingredients

- 1 cup self-raising flour
- 1/2 cup plain flour
- 2 tsp ground cinnamon
- 150 g butter chopped
- 3/4 cup brown sugar firmly packed
- 0.6 cup rolled oats
- 8 apples
- 1 tbs cinnamon sugar optional for dusting

Direction

- Preheat oven to 180C fan-forced. Lightly grease a baking dish.
- Combine the flours and cinnamon in a food processor. Add the butter and process in short bursts until the mixture resembles coarse breadcrumbs. Transfer to a bowl. Stir in the brown sugar and oats, use fingers to mix until crumble almost comes together.
- Cut 1cm off the top of the apples. Remove the core. Use a teaspoon to scoop out apple to about halfway, leaving a 1cm border around the edge. Place the apples into the baking dish, press crumble mixture (about 1/3 cup per apple) into the well and evenly over the apples.
- Bake for 30 minutes or until apples are just tender and the crumble is golden.
- Serve warm and dusted with cinnamon sugar or cold as a lunch box/after-school snack

Index

A

Amaretti 3,10,18

Apple 3,5,6,7,8,11,12,13,14,15,16,17,19,21,23,24

B

Banana 3,8,9

Berry 3,10,23

Blueberry 3,11

Bran 1,2

Brill 3,11

C

Cake 3,5,8,13,17

Caramel 3,12

Cinnamon 3,13

Coconut 3,13

Cream 11,17

Crumble 1,3,4,5,6,7,8,9,10,11,12,13,14,15,16,17,18,19,20,21,22,23,24

Custard 3,5,7,10,12,14

F

Fruit 3,15,18,23

H

Heart 3,5

L

Lemon 3,16,17

Lime 3,17

M

Mascarpone 3,10,18

Mince 3,15

N

Nut 4,23,24

O

Oats 3,7

Orange 3,18

P

Peach 3,15,18,19,20

Pear 3,9,13

Pecan 3,12,17

Peel 8,9,11,12,15,21,24

Pineapple 3,4

Plum 3,10,20

R

Raspberry 3,20

Rhubarb 3,14,21

S

Stew 5,15,17

Strawberry 3,22

Syrup 3,7

T

Tea 3,11

W

Walnut 3,7

Conclusion

Thank you again for downloading this book!

I hope you enjoyed reading about my book!

If you enjoyed this book, please take the time to share your thoughts and post a review on Amazon. It'd be greatly appreciated!

Write me an honest review about the book – I truly value your opinion and thoughts and I will incorporate them into my next book, which is already underway.

Thank you!

If you have any questions, **feel free to contact at:** *author@chardrecipes.com*

Brandy Farr

chardrecipes.com

Printed in Great Britain
by Amazon